Cosmic Mesa

Armando Batista

Copyright © 2021 by Armando Batista
All rights reserved.

DWA Press is an Imprint of Dominican Writers Assoc., a 501 (c)(3) non-profit literary arts organization founded in 2015 with the mission to support Dominican writers by providing them the tools and resources to become published authors.

All rights reserved.
No part of this book may be reproduced or transmitted in any form or by any means, electronic or mechanical, including photocopying, recording, or by an information storage and retrieval system-- except by a reviewer who may quote brief passages in a review to be printed in a magazine or newspaper—without permission in writing from the holder of the copyright. Please do not participate or encourage piracy of copyright materials in violation of the author's rights. Purchase only authorized editions.

Editor: JP Infante
Cover Art Design: Armando Batista
Book Design: Angela Abreu
ISBN-978-1-7372467-2-5

Published in the United States.

DWA Press
An imprint of Dominican Writers Assoc.
www.dominicanwriters.com
info@dominicanwriters.com

In *Cosmic Mesa,* Armando Batista maps out for us a funky, "electro cappuccino," "blacker than dark matter" mythopolis where a "heart beats like Taiko drums." These poems will nourish you like "salchicha, queso frito, mangú" so slide on your space suit and let them guide you to a memory palace you might never want to leave.

--Tomás Q. Morín, author of *Machete*

The activating mind of Armando Batista puts forth a dynamic, experimental installation of poems. Language cannot survive in the shape it is presented and so Batista changes their shapes and recalibrates them from their original Latin/African wombs giving poetry and poetics a new language to live by.

--Parneshia Jones, author of *Vessel*

Armando Batista's poetry collection tells the story of a Dominican-York traveling through space and time as their past and Caribbean history unravels before them. This collection is an archipelago, made up of sci-fi and memoir poems told in a voice fractured by who they were, who they've become, and the horizon at the end of the road.

--JP Infante, author of *On the Tip of Your Mother's Tongue*

When colonizers burn your history, you piece it together through family, stories, and ancestors. You delve into their memory palace, and/or you map-make. Armando Batista does this and more in his debut chapbook. Identity, transformation, gentrification, and elegy are all up for inspection, and Batista is relentless in his introspection. Come, open to the first page, and fall in.

--Roberto Carlos Garcia, author of *[Elegies]*

Batista's Cosmic Mesa is a celebration of hybridity. Packed with color and movement, these intimate verses reflect the countless cultural intersections that map one's identity. With an interstellar blend of Afrofuturism, spoken word, and more conventional forms of Western poetry, Batista's speaker dances through space and time. He provides readers with an atlas for boldly crossing borders into new conceptions of being.

--Donald Quist, author of *For Other Ghosts & To Those Bounded*

For Heriberta Batista Ramirez Acosta
"Abuela"
1923-2019

map-making

The map terraforms, with peaks and valleys outlined
by the blood of my ancestors. Turn to page 1491
to know them before Columbus.

This map originates in my future mother and father,
before they knew of hidden treasure; it starts
in the Dominican Republic: Eastern part of the island
first known as Ayiti/Kiskeya to the indigenous Tainos;
Haiti/primo of the western divide; shared blood runs deep
with ambivalence. Turn to page 1844 to know how
Utopia was.

The key(s): cassava, guava, brown skin, and virtuous
hips/
drumming out rhythm of Afro codex: la tambora. (see
perico ripiao)

The key(s): Language/ferried through imperialist teeth
to the ears of settlers on other stolen shores- Barbakoa,
Hamaka, Hurakan. Turn to the pages of your Oxford
English to find our stolen treasure.

The map re-forms in New York circa 1979, stretched out
on the vientre of the woman who would become
my mother; I'm the 4th X. Turn to page 2016
to know my beautiful struggle with art and commerce.

She and my future father have to figure out how to locate
empty bellies and unearth hidden dreams, with limited
instrumentation. Turn to page 1993 to see how I stole
my blessing.

Manhattan's map was also formed by una tortuga carrying
the Algonquin nation on her mothering back.

Turn to page 1626 to learn how these rich/varied/
starved/divided/fighting/spiritual people
were duped at their own game of trade.
Stolen in translation. (see serpent's tongue.)

The key: *Map,* a poem by Wislawa Szymborska,
circa 2014. Said to be her last. In it, she flattens
our world. The one we carry in our desires.
My favorite line confirms my own desirous nature
for redrawing my world:

I like maps because they lie.

Naming

> *The future enters into us,*

Mami
holds fetal me inside her
futures my naming from a telenovela
A_____? dark skinned sinister hunk one-liner macho
A_____? light skinned angelic one-liner macho

Why she chose the villain's name I may never know

> *in order to transform itself in us,*

This poem as X
roots itself in the doorway
like winter frost so light can enter

> *long before it happens.*
> *-Rilke*

She futured
word into flesh an unknowable me
~~I wish to~~ melt away X

Rotten Fruit Philosophy

"Bite that piece off. The rest is good to eat."
Momma knows best.

To the worm residing in that mushy sector
it was room and board.

I bite into the apple and spit out the "bad" part.

I didn't ask the worm
I didn't research property rights or make a bid
on the apple estate; maybe the worm would've shared.

I take what I want, only hesitating when I saw
the *phylum annelida* burrowed in my apple.
My apple. My apple.

If only the Lenape could've spit out the founding èmigrès
who came and took their Mannahatta,
though they never would've said it was *theirs*.
If asked, they probably would've shared...

Wish our apartment was really ours.
Wish my pop's car was really his.
Wish my time was really mine.
Wish I didn't feel like that earth-
worm:
        dis/
           /placed.

Morir Soñando: An Elegy for Heriberta Batista

Berta
Murio soñando...
Night your cloak
Descanse

Berta
Choose your home: Amongst the stars
coral of El Rio Aguila
faraway islands forgotten by conquest
where ancestors hold un lugar at la cosmic mesa
for you

Heriberta Batista Ramirez Acosta
Your name stays on my childhood lips
and I sing your hymns:
One part jugo Tropicana
One part leche
A spoonful of azuca blanca
served over ice in a tall crystal glass;
un morir soñando resurrects my childhood bliss

Abuela would make me
desayunos
tres golpes of island-born love:
Salchicha, queso frito, mangú, huevo frito
y morir soñando to wash it all down

Later I discover
these desayunos were postcards postmarked with desire
landing me in the land of our elders;
more than just a spring break destination.

Berta left
in her cloak of midnight hidden messages:

La vida no es facil, mijo
The philosophy of longevity
Tu eres un muchachito muy inteligente
A love supreme
Trujillo se me pego a la falda, y aca
Traje su demonios
Post Banana Republic Syndrome
Dios perdona a todo
A god that eases reality
Eta ciudad me jode los huesos
Surviving city winters
No te olvida de donde tu eres
Dropping seeds of roots remembrance
Ay, mijo. Que nunca te pase a ti; Tu papa...
Es buen hombre, tampoco facil
Two sons buried before burying her
and one who corrected the imbalance

Berta
soñaste a good way to die
your cloak of night/mare galloped
old-timers/springing your soul into dream's country:
dance   draw   sing

I been meaning to ask you: Why did you wait so long?
To which you answer in a language
I have no reference for...yet

                        but I do feel my heart beating
                           in your soul's hands, 'Buela

Candela

That's how Abuelo bit it: liver gave out. The brown sugar
stopped processing in his processor. Was it Wild Turkey
or Old Grand-Dad's he sipped on? I remember
the sweet caramel smell that permeated from him;
a handsome Indio with mustard for the whites of his eyes.
He had a batmobile station wagon, ala Adam West but
only in cognitive dissonance, red fins and bucket leather
seats. We'd ride down Riverside Drive with his two
doberman pinschers in the back seats, their big ol' heads
out the windows, tongues swinging. I think Ibrahim Ferrer
was playing on the cassette deck *Candela, candela,
candela me queme aé* but that could be me wishful
thinking or conflating the brown sugar men, who both
wore embroidered golf caps. There's that, and the dollar
bill origami shirt he, Wenselao Ramon Batista, made
and framed for me.

Later, I used the money to buy a toy of no particular
importance: I fucked up.

The gift of memory still haunts me
Like everytime I slide a stack of $1 bills on the bar
after sipping on some brown sugar:
Is this your dollar, Abuelo?
Or, this one?

Anagram

*a word or phrase made by rearranging the letters of
another word or phrase; word-play; a method to find
hidden messages, and other selves.*

Armando
Spanish derivative of the German *Herman*
Hari- army   Army man

Was it fate or chance that I'd poem on a war ship at 18
taking arms against a sea of troubles   and by opposing
become trouble—browner and slicker than your avg
grunt—late onset genius kicked in after dreams
of becoming a SEAL shattered

I matter as far as I can throw a box
or keep the brig warm
I matter-of-factly lost my marbles to gain my freedom

And still the soldiering-on creases never hid my sorrow
books became portals, ideas spread and infect me

I twist and turn to be released from duty   reach
the end; my sentence as sailor is no more

I must become something other than my namesake
rearrange reality to fit artistic wings
take to the road manned
with will regret passion ambition

my remixed consciousness: Roadman

Stoned
after Carlos Drummond Andrade

Roadman trips on a stone
in the middle of a rough and dusty road.
Watch where you're goin' grumbles the rough stone.
Roadman apologizes to the rough and lonely stone,
looking to avoid a dramatic event;
with weary toes and crow's feet retinas
travelling too many a rough and dusty road
alone, he turns/towards the rough and lonely stone:
Wanna roll with me? pointing down the road
appealing to the core of the rough and ready stone.

A.I.R.
I'm gonna send him to outerspace, to find another race
-Chase The Devil

Space   the final frontier… reached
Arteest In Resiidance
Kosmos kin
landing on drum pads
licking reed with stardust
settling in for a long space stay-tion

A.I.R. Apparent
residing amongst my arkestry // constellation orchestral
studio phonic grooves // moon beams // anti-gravity
lifting up musicology to a natural infinitude
I, Sun Ra solar flare furious funk
        compose quasi chords
        meteorize melodies
        reverb galactic verses   back to Planet Earth

I ain't forget ya. Hope ya ain't forget me

In this What-If? I, Sun Ra, flip historical rejection,
NASA accepts my black ass genius

Go! Nasa exclaims   *zooom   EnGagE   we in Houston*
have yet to truly embrace human

                              infinitesimal
                                  -ness

        You, Sun Ra, must take on the mantle and become
                                Astro Black

Astro Black/mythology/Astro Black/blacker than dark matter/scattered across known and unknown universe(s)/Astro Black/mythology/*The Universe is in my voice*   bounce to anti-gravity rhythm   bounce to the bebop in my space suit   double bounce pass the moon,   untethered
planetary matters *roll into a* sub-atomic ball and *spinnnnn* faster than the speed of light//sound//signals/back as I's

                          s

                      p

                        i

                            n

                                o

                             u

                          t

        into

((((INTERSTELLAR))))
  ((((SPACE))))

     and

     the

  ----B----
  e a t
  o n

Mythopolis

future ones

        Upon visit
        stop by the tree
        in the middle of the ruined city

        Elsewhere
        roots shoot thru   grey slabs   to breathe

        Find me
        tipping (trippin') over a rusted can:
        Café Bustelo

        my nose in the dark hollow
        tiene que ser bueno
        inhaling the phantom roast

        From the cra/ck'd
        a branched cherry carrying childhood:
        little fingers dip
        pan de aqua
        into a tin cup full of oro

Memory Palace

1

I open my eyes
in this strange body– purple eye lashes
unfurl my vision onto a room whose walls
are made of tall grass
The bed is made of the ocean's crystal tears
the sheets are of chocolate whip cream
and I breathe in the fragrance of ginger
I move these limbs/crow wings blue/black feathers flap
making waves on the grassy walls
A leaf of grass escapes

I walk this mostly pink Himalayan Mountain salt body
down a playground slide to the first floor, or
is it the fifth? If memory serves rite
Numbers are ceremonies celebrating chaos' invitation
to try and figure out the formula of everything

2

Somewhere a mother has prepared her child's
favorite dish while this body's olfactory is pumping
clouds of sancocho into me
Satellites spin on the jester's trained hands
sending signals to the Ministry of Childhood:
Children wearing the Sun's skin in a hoodie
are magicians to be protected by Peace Keepers

A mother, not unlike the one who cooked the sancocho

sings a sweet hymn from her xylophone vocal chords
of longing for her babies to stay babies
and not be bashed by the world's misshaped hand
The chorus of albino hairless mice harmonize
and the chapel of abandoned socks join in

3

I take flight with these blue/black wings through the ruins
of Lego blocks
stumble onto a couch made of spaghetti knots
where B. Lee and M. Ali are having their long awaited
exhibition over a game of marbles—
Be formless, shapeless, like water
Float like a butterfly, sting like a bee
Clak clak go the masterful attacks Clakity clak
marbles containing galaxies upon galaxies, dead legends
Waha!-ing/*Young Man, Rumble!*-ing
begin a new world, destroy another

I outstretch these pink claws to stay a little longer
but begin to sink into the spaghetti couch
These sea salt limbs detach to provide flavor
and I float

Outside of an aquarium car
the driver a shape-shifting octopus spinnin'
golden age MC's
Once upon a time not long ago
I sink into the paper like I was ink
Nothin's equivalent to a New York State of Mind
Schools of pizza slices swim past subjects

they've already mastered:
Afro-Atlantic Musiaquology
Hermit Crab Leadership
Black Hole Swing Dance
Driverless Fractal Sight Seeing

I am enjoying all of this without a body
of my own to hold onto

How different is it to make up a memory
that seems unlikely than to remember
something that is no longer there?
I mean *there there*
There, there

Chronesthesia
is the technical term for the brain's ability to maintain simultaneous awareness of past, present and future and to travel back and forth between them.

The boy, age 8, lays on his stomach on his bed in a darkened room. The only light is coming from the tube—it has an antenna on top, like an outer space device. VHF/UHF channel knobs. There is a *Twilight Zone* Marathon on WPIX Channel 11. It is New York 1987. The boy appears statuesque, a bronze cast of a resting youth—chin on open palms, blanket creates a shield/hood/defense system in case the episode(s) get(s) really scary (which it will.) The youngest of four, left alone to his own solitary consignment. He is the baby *who gets away with everything* his second oldest brother says. He gets away with a lot. But that will change.

Rod Serling's voice speaks from the tube: "You unlock this door with the key of imagination. Beyond it is another dimension—a dimension of sound, a dimension of sight, a dimension of mind. You're moving into a land of both shadow and substance, of things and ideas. You've just crossed over into the Twilight Zone."

> *A safe place. These eyes*
> *this imagination. A place to rest*
> *a moment to catch   breath*

The boy is afraid and excited all at once.

> *Note: Afraid. Excitable*
> *The sound of drumming*

His heart beats like Taiko drums. He jumps up right between the intro and the fade-in into the first episode, dismantling his helmet/shield/defense system to open the bedroom door just slightly, so the hallway light bleeds in.

> *Note: Illumination. Across dark time. Note: We/re Still here*

Less scary.
He re-positions. Grabs his soggy Frosted Flakes bowl. Assumes the phantom crunch;
He's in.

> *"They're Grrreat." Re-member wonder. This is light Stay a little longer Keep the light*

But the breeze moves thru

HouseHead Chronicles

HouseHead thumps down foot four to the floor
throws up hands, circles expand/up/in space

HouseHead sweats waterfalls cleansing
robotic work hours

Timed spins with vinyl: Africa Bambataa to
Dinah Washington to MJ to Prince to

a Frankie Knuckles classic, sweat on four drips
to the floor

HouseHead slides and glides gyrates contact improv with other house/heads bouncing

hearts/bumping spirits lifted, utopia
in the fourth dimension

Freedom in a broken down basement/

RED light illuminates a "Back in Da Day"
New York: Alphabet City, Loisada,

Boogie Down, Spanish Harlem, Da Heights
The four sssslows
DJ winding down the gyrating vinyl

HouseHead's heartbeat still beats out four
chambers synchronize in the 4th dimension

Feats groov floor 2 ceiling 2 make-believing
HseHds float up/stars into night's stairs

Beats to beat back next Days' robo tick
tock

HsHd finds a late-night pizza joint
slice of nostalgia

Silverchrome Chariot awaits
the gallop home

Tick
Tock
haunts the city

Slumber settles The Beat into memoria
treasured deep in hips, ankles, spine

4 2 4lr unlocks from the chambered pump
and whispers deep in the bones *Girl,*
I'll house you

  Girl, I'll house you
  Girl, I'll house you
  You in my hut now, don't you know?

while waiting for the beast
to dispense the electro cappuccino.

Aging

Pain between my knuckles, now that I am older.
My youth's escaping me now that I am older.

A mother watches her 2-year-old strumming his
father's guitar. Tears falling: *My lil' man's older.*

Branches blow in windy cities/roots dig in deeper.
Cannot be gentrified: *Always, I am older.*

Will earth implode or explode?
Science doubts/Gods don't know...
Journeys 'round the
sun: *We are all engrams older.*

Skyscrapers scrape the sky, subways block out sunshines.
Hustle for hustle's sake/NY's not mine... damn, older.

Roadman backpacks once more/weary traveler.
His solace: *Time'll finish me when I am elder.*

Acknowledgements

Acknowledgement is made to the following journals where some of these poems have appeared:

CRACKEN Mexican lit zine: "Rotten Fruit Philosophy" (translated by David Anuar González)

Death Rattle: "Rotten Fruit Philosophy"
Death Rattle: "Mythopolis"

Ni De Aquí, Ni De Allá anthology (Dominican Writers Association's): "Candela"

I also want to thank a couple of folks who were instrumental in helping put out this chapbook:

JP Infante, thank you brother for your editing superpowers, your encouragement and support in helping me shape this book. I look forward to working with you on the next one;-)

Angy Abreu and Dominican Writers Assoc., mil gracias for saying yes to publishing my "poetic mixtape." I am honored to be a part of the growing platano canon!

My advisors at VCFA— Tomás Q. Morín, Parneshia Jones, Nance Van Winckel, Patricia Smith, Bob Vivan, Harrison Candelaria Fletcher. Your guidance, encouragement, cheerleading, firm and gentle challenges and questions allowed me to see my poetics more clearly and bring it to the next level.

A mi mama y mi papa, Bethania y Vicente Batista. Amor infinito.

Author's Bio

Armando Batista is a poet, performer and educator. He earned his M.F.A. in Writing from Vermont College of Fine Arts, and a B.A. in Theater from Temple University.

Armando's poetry has been translated and published in the Mexican literary journal *CRACKEN* and is forthcoming in the Mexican publication *Pliego16, Death Rattle/OROBORO* and Dominican Writers Association's anthology *Ni De Aquí, Ni De Allá.* His essays are published in the online journals *past-ten, The Maine Review,* and *The Abstract Elephant Magazine.* He is currently working on a poetry collection and a travel memoir. *Cosmic Mesa* is his debut chapbook. Follow him on Instagram: @armando_batista_poet

Photo Credit: Emmanuel Abreu

www.ingramcontent.com/pod-product-compliance
Lightning Source LLC
Chambersburg PA
CBHW072210100526
44589CB00015B/2468